AN HECHE BOOK

THE UNTOLD STORY

EN MAX PRESS

Copyright@2022

ALL RIGHTS RESERVED

TABLE OF CONTENTS

THE BIOGRAPHY

PART ONE

THE EARLY LIFE OF ANNE

PART TWO

CAREER LIFE

AWARDS AND ACHIEVEMENTS

PART THREE

PERSONAL LIFE

- Richard Burgi (1987 – 1991)
- Steve Martin (1994 – 1997)
- Ellen DeGeneres (1997 – 2001)
- Coley Laffoon (2001 – 2007)
- James Tupper (2007 – 2018)
- Thomas Jane
- Lindsey Adams Buckingham

CAR CRASH AND HEALTH UPDATE

PART FOUR

MORE OF ANNE

LEGAL BATTLES

CHARITY WORKS

LAST NOTE

ANNE HECHE

THE BIOGRAPHY

Anne Heche is a well-known American actress who was introduced to the world of entertainment by the daytime soap opera known as "Another World." Heche was born on May 25, 1969, in the United States. She is famous for being in a relationship with the well-known comedian Ellen DeGeneres. In addition to that, she has also written scripts and directed films. In 1998, People magazine named the 50 most beautiful people in the world, and she was included on that list. Donald Joe Hache, Anne's father, was born in 1938 and passed away on March 3, 1983 in New York, United States. He was born in the United States. Nancy Heche, the actress's mother, is a prominent American activist. At this time, Nancy Heche has 85 years under her belt. The 10th of March, 1937 was the day she was born. Her siblings are as follows; Cynthia, who was born on August

26, 1961 and passed away on October 26, 1961; Nate, who was born on April 21, 1965, and passed away on June 4, 1983; Abigail who is a jewelry designer; Susan who is an author. Before he passed away from AIDS, Anne had accused her father of having sexual relations with her when she was a child.

As they stood by her father, her mother, and her lone surviving sister, Abigail distanced themselves from her. This caused a rift in her relationship with her mother and sister. She has made appearances in a number of films and television shows, including "I Know What You Did Last Summer," "Fatal Desire," "The Brave," "Wild Side," and "Walking and Talking." During the course of her career, her romantic relationship with Ellen DeGeneres was the subject of widespread controversy. After that, she tied the knot with Coley Laffoon, but they eventually divorced. After that, she began an intimate relationship with James Tupper, with whom she eventually had a second child. She has published a book titled 'Call Me Crazy: A Memoire,' which is an account of her turbulent life, including her abusive father and her lesbian relationship. After she ended her relationship with Ellen DeGeneres, she struggled with a variety of mental and emotional problems, some of which required her to seek professional help. The connection between actress Anne Heche and James Tupper and Coleman Laffoon resulted in the birth of their two children. The two kids are referred to as Atlas Heche Tupper and Homer Laffoon. Anne Heche and ex-James Tupper are Atlas Heche Tupper's parents. Since he was born in 2009, he will be thirteen years old in the year 2022. Heche and her ex-husband, Coleman Laffoon, raised their son Homer Laffoon together. He was born in Los Angeles, California, in the

United States on March 2, 2002, which means that he will be 20 years old in the year 2022.

The recent car accident that left Anne Heche intubated at a hospital after suffering severe burns is the latest in a long line of controversies that have dogged her throughout the years. Anne Heche has had a troubled career as well as a troubled personal life. It has been reported that the actress, who is 53 years old, is in a "stable condition," and her family and friends have asked for "thoughts and prayers." However, it has also emerged that she made some concerning comments shortly before the crash, which left her "lucky to be alive." This article includes information on Anne Heche's age, her biography, her children, her marriage, her parents, her husband, and a great deal more.

PART ONE

THE EARLY LIFE OF ANNE

Anne Heche was the youngest of five children to be born to Nancy Heche (nee Prickett) and Donald Joseph Heche. Heche was born on May 25, 1969, in Aurora, Ohio. During her childhood, Heche and her family moved a total of eleven times; at one point, they lived in an Amish community. In response to a question about her father's line of work that was posed to her in an interview that aired on Larry King Live in 2001, Heche stated that her father was a choir director. On the other hand, she stated that she did not believe he made a significant amount of money on that per week. She claimed that her father always maintained the story that he worked in the oil and gas industry right up until the day he passed away. However, he was never a part of the gas and oil trade at any point in time.

When Heche was twelve years old, her family made Ocean City, New Jersey, their permanent home. Anne's financial situation was so precarious that she found work in Swanton at a dinner theater. During an interview, she made a statement in which she stated that at that time, they had been kicked out of their house and that her family was holed up living in a bedroom in the home of a generous family from her church. She said that she and her family were living in this bedroom because they had no other place to go. She was making more money than anyone else in her family, with weekly take-home pay of one hundred dollars. After living together for a year, they decided it was time to strike out on their own, so they put all of their savings into a single envelope and hid it away.

Heche's father, who was 45 years old at the time of his death, passed away on March 3,

1983, from AIDs. Even though he never admitted to being a homosexual, and remained in a state of complete denial right up until the day he passed away, there was talk that he contracted the illness through his homosexual relationships. Anne claimed that she didn't think it was just one because he was a very promiscuous man, and they were familiar with his lifestyle back then. In spite of the fact that her father was gay, Heche claims that he sexually abused her from the time she was an infant until she was 12 years old, giving her genital herpes as a result. During an interview in 2001 with The Advocate, Heche was asked, "But why would a gay man rape a girl?" Her response was that she didn't think he was just a gay man. She shared her perspective, in which she described him as sexually deviant. She stated that she had always been led to believe that her father was gay and that he hid the fact for professional reasons. She also did not believe that he was sexually abusive toward her. More and more, he was unable to be who he was, and as a result, more and more of that came out of him in the ways that it did.

As a result of the events that have transpired in their lives, Anne and her mother Nancy, who is now 85 years old, do not communicate with one another. In point of fact, Nancy has never even spoken to either of Homer and Atlas, Anne's two children. It is said that Nancy, a woman who is highly pious and who is dedicated to her husband, did not support her daughter Anne in the past. She went on to have a career as an activist and a motivational speaker after having a falling out with her daughter and experiencing the death of her husband. In 1997, Anne began a relationship with the well-known comedian Ellen Degeneres. When Nancy found out about it, she felt as though it was an insult to their faith.

To add to this, she is a firm believer that homosexuals can be reformed, and she has made this the focus of her entire life, as evidenced by the campaigns she runs and the speeches she gives.

PART TWO
CAREER LIFE

• She got her start in the entertainment industry with a part in the daytime soap opera "Another World," for which she was nominated for a Daytime Emmy Award in the category of "Outstanding Younger Actress in a Drama Series" in the year 1991. She made her debut in a feature film the following year with a role as Mary Jane in Disney's "The Adventures of Huck Finn." She first appeared on screen in the television movie "O Pioneers," which was produced by the Hallmark Hall of Fame and broadcast in 1992.

• She was a college student when she landed her first major role in the movie "If These Walls Could Talk," in which she appeared alongside Cher and Demi Moore. This was her breakthrough performance. Her work in the movie "Walking and Talking" was praised, and the movie itself was included on "Entertainment Weekly's" list of the Top 50 Cult Films of All Time because of her performance in the movie.

• During this time, she had a fleeting romantic relationship with her co-star from the film "A Simple Twist of Fate," Steve Martin. Their romance took place off-screen.

• She went on to perform in films such as "Wag the Dog," a political satire, and "Volcano," a disaster film, opposite actors such as Robert De Niro, Dustin Hoffman, and Tommy Lee Jones. Despite the fact that she played supporting roles in these movies, many reviewers believed she had much more potential than that.

• In 1998, she made her debut in the romantic adventure film titled "Six Days, Seven Nights," starring opposite Harrison Ford. This was her first leading role. The actress's same-sex relationship with Ellen DeGeneres, which was brought to light around the same time as the movie's release, was likely a contributing factor to the movie's lack of consensus among critics.

• Before making her debut on Broadway in the Pulitzer Prize-winning play 'Proof' in 2002, for which she received positive reviews, she appeared in a number of television serials and television films. Her performances in these roles were well received. Her acting in the Broadway show 'Twentieth Century' earned her a nomination for the Tony Award in the category of 'Best Actress in a Play,' and her performance in the 2004 film 'Gracie's Choice' was recognized with a nomination for the Primetime Emmy Award in the category of 'Best Supporting Actress.'

• In 2006, she launched her own series under the title "Men in Trees," but the show was canceled the following year due to a strike among the writers. She continued to make appearances in sex comedies and horror shows such as "Suffering Men's Charity" and "Spread" on television.

• Among her most recent projects are the motion pictures "My Friend Dahmer" and "Armed Response," as well as the television war series "The Brave" (2017 - 2018). In addition to that, she has provided her voice for the video game titled "9: The Last Resort" and directed several episodes of various television series.

• She has been a regular guest on the television show 'Everwood' and co-hosted the weekly radio show on SiriusXM called 'Love and Hache' with Jason Ellis. The show was called "Love and Hache."

AWARDS AND ACHIEVEMENTS

AWARDS	YEAR	CATEGORY	PROJECT
Soap Opera Digest Awards [Winner]	1989	Outstanding Female Newcomer: Daytime	Another World (1964)
Daytime Emmy Awards [Nominee]	1989	Outstanding Juvenile Female in a Drama Series	Another World (1964)
Daytime Emmy Awards [Winner]	1991	Outstanding Younger Actress in a Drama Series	Another World (1964)
Soap Opera Digest Awards [Winner]	1992	Outstanding Lead Actress	Another World (1964)

National Board of Review Awards [Winner]	1997	Best Supporting Actress	Donnie Brasco (1997) Wag the Dog (1997)
Golden Satellite Awards [Nominee]	1998	Best Actress in a Supporting role in a motion Picture, Comedy or Musical	Wag the Dog (1997)
Stinker Award [Winner]	1998	Worst Actress	Psycho (1998) Six Days Seven Nights (1998)

Razzie Award [Nominee]	1999	Worst Actress	Psycho (1998)
Fangoria Chainsaw Award [Nominee]	1999	Best Supporting Actress	Psycho (1998)
Blockbuster Entertainment Award [Nominee]	1999	Favorite Actress-Comedy/Romance	Six Days Seven Nights (1998)
Saturn Award [Nominee]	1999	Best Supporting Actress	Psycho (1998)
Women in Film Lucy Awards	2000		

[Winner]			
Audience Award [Winner]	2000	Best Film	If These Walls Could Talk 2 (2000)
GLAAD Media Awards Stephen F. Kolzak Award	2000		
Csapnivalo Awards Golden State [Nominee]	2000	Best Actress in a Leading Role	Return to Paradise (1998)
Primetime Emmy Awards	2004	Outstanding Supporting	Gracie's Choice

[Nominee]		Actress in a Miniseries or a Movie	(1994)
Saturn Award [Nominee]	2005	Best Actress on Television	The Dead Will Tell (2004)
Prism Awards [Nominee]	2005	Performance in a TV movie or Miniseries	Gracie's Choice (2004)
BTVA People's Choice Voice Acting Awards [Winner]	2015	Best Vocal Ensemble in a Television Series- Action/Drama	The Legend of Korra (2012)
BTVA Television Voice Acting	2015	Best Vocal Ensemble in a Television Series-	The Legend of Korra

Award [Nominee]		Action/Drama	(2012)
Career Achievement Award [Winner]	2019		

PART THREE

PERSONAL LIFE

A great number of people are discussing the romantic lives and connections of famous people. People all over the world who are obsessed with their favorite celebrities look to it as their primary source of information about those celebrities. A variety of media outlets, which uncover and report on a wide range of information, keep fans up to date on the personal lives of their celebrity idols by uncovering and reporting on a wide variety of information. It seems that despite the fact that many of these famous people have attempted to restrict the level of intrusion that the media has into their private lives, they have been unsuccessful. This is likely because of the speed with which and the extent to which information about them is disseminated. Some of these celebrities have been able to avoid being discovered by the media thanks to their limited presence on social media; however, other celebrities have been unaffected by the rumors that circulate on the internet. Anne Heche is just one of a long list of celebrities who, in an attempt to shield their private lives from the scrutiny of the media, have been unsuccessful. Over the course of the past few years, she has been in relationships with multiple men. Reports indicate that Anne Heche has been in at least 9 relationships in her past. This topic has also been brought up in conversations with her devoted followers.

- **Richard Burgi (1987 - 1991)**

Richard Burgi dated Anne Heche in the past, but their relationship did not continue for very long because it ultimately ended in failure. Richard William Burgi is an American film and television actor who was born on July 30, 1958. He is best known for playing the role of Detective Jim

Ellison on the television show The Sentinel and Karl Mayer on the television show Desperate Housewives. Richard Burgi's current spouse is Lori Kahn, and they have two children together.

- **Steve Martin (1994 – 1997)**

After the termination of her previous relationship, Anne started dating comedian and actor Steve Martin. American actor, comedian, writer, director, and musician Stephen Glenn Martin is well-known in his field. On August 14, 1945, he entered this world. He was born in the United States. Writer for The Smothers Bros Comedy Hour in the 1960s, Martin became well-known for his contributions to the show. Then he became well-known for being a frequent visitor to Johnny Carson's The Tonight Show. During the 1970s, Martin took his offbeat, absurdist comedy routines on the road across the country, where he performed for sold-out crowds. Since the 1980s, Emmys and other accolades attest to Martin's accomplishment as an actor, writer, dramatist, pianist, and banjo player... The list also includes the Grammy, and the American Comedy Award, amongst other accolades. Martin began his career in comedy but has since branched out into other fields. In 2004, Martin was placed at number six on a list of the 100 greatest stand-up comedians that was compiled by Comedy Central. At the 5th Annual Governors Awards that were held by the Academy in 2013, he was presented with an Honorary Academy Award. While he started playing the banjo at an early age and has always included music in his comedy performances, since the 2000s he has committed most of his professional life to music, acting less and devoting much of his time playing the banjo, filming, and traveling with other bluegrass outfits. A 2002 Grammy for Best Country Instrumental Performance was shared with one of these artists, Earl Scruggs.

Ever since the turn of the millennium, he has focused his career on music. In 2009, he released his first album under his own name, titled The Crow: New Songs for the 5-String Banjo. The album was nominated for a Grammy Award and ultimately won the award for Best Bluegrass Album. The couple dated for a total of two years before deciding to officially end their relationship in 1997.

Ellen DeGeneres (1997 - 2001)

It was Heche's relationship with Ellen DeGeneres that made her newsworthy in the tabloids in the 1990s. Heche and DeGeneres, both 64 years old at the time, were together from 1997 until August of 2000, and at one point in their relationship, they even stated that they would enter into a civil union in the state of Vermont if that were to become a legal option there. American comedian, talk show presenter, actor, writer, and producer Ellen Lee

DeGeneres. The United States is the place of her birth on January 26, 1958. She played the title role in the sitcom Ellen from 1994 until 1998, and since 2003, she has been the host of her own syndicated talk show on television, titled The Ellen DeGeneres Show. Her career as a stand-up comedian began in the early 1980s, and one of her early performances was broadcast on The Tonight Show with Johnny Carson in 1986. As a film actress, Ellen DeGeneres has starred in the movies The Love Letter, Mr. Wrong, and EDtv. She also voiced Dory in the Finding Nemo (2003) and Finding Dory 2016 Disney/Pixar animated features (2016), For Nemo, she was honored with the Saturn Award for Best Supporting Actress, which was the first time an actress won a Saturn Award for a voice performance. Finding Dory (2016) is the sequel During the ninth season of American Idol, which aired in 2010, she participated as a judge.

The couple has never provided a definitive explanation for why they decided to end their relationship; however, at the time of the breakup, a source told the Daily News that the relationship had simply "run its course" due to the fact that it wasn't functioning well. The actresses issued a statement to the publication in which they informed the audience that, sadly, they had come to the conclusion that they needed to put an end to their romantic involvement with one another. According to them, it was a friendly breakup, and they looked back on the three and a half years that they had spent together as some of the most meaningful years of their lives. During the trying time, they strongly requested that others respect their need for privacy. It was reported that hours after the breakup, Heche was taken away in an ambulance to the hospital after she knocked on the door of a stranger in central California. She was reportedly babbling incoherently the entire time she was being transported. While she was being driven, she could be heard saying that she was not crazy. Heche later told ABC News about the incident, describing life as crazy and claiming that she was raised in a crazy family and that it took 31 years to get the crazy out of her.

• Coley Laffoon (2001 - 2007)

Reportedly, Heche ended her relationship with DeGeneres for cameraman Coley Laffoon, whom she had met in the year 2000 while DeGeneres was on her stand-up comedy tour. Heche and Laffoon tied the knot on September 1st, 2001. Anne Heche and her ex-husband, the cameraman Coley Laffoon, were married for a total of six years, and during that time, they welcomed a son whom they named Homer. In 2007, Heche filed for divorce from her husband, but due to the contentious nature of the court battle, the divorce was not finalized until 2009, two years after Heche's initial filing.

• James Tupper (2007 - 2018)

It was rumored that Anne Heche divorced her husband at the time, Coley Laffoon, in order to be with her co-star in the film "Men in Trees," James Tupper, whom she began dating in 2007. James Tupper is a Canadian actor who was born on August 4, 1965. He is best known for his roles as Jack Slattery on the television series Men in Trees (which aired on ABC), Dr. Chris Sands on the NBC medical drama series Mercy, and David Clarke on the television series Revenge (which aired on ABC). In addition, he played a leading role in the post-apocalyptic drama Aftermath, which aired on Space in Canada and Syfy in the United States. He is the main character in the current season of the HBO series Big Little Lies. On December 5, 2008, a representative for Heche announced that the actress was expecting their first child, a son, who would be her second child and his first. Atlas Heche Tupper is the couple's only child together. After many happy years together, Tupper and Heche decided to go their separate ways in 2018. Anne believed that healthy relationships evolve and develop over time, and she and her partner had given themselves ample opportunity to do so. They had a great deal of affection for one another and intended to continue cultivating love and harmony in the upbringing of their two handsome sons.

- **Thomas Jane**

Between the years 2019 and 2021, Anne Heche was dating Thomas Jane. Before they started dating, they were each other's best friends, and they took pleasure in spending time together. They were featured in an article that was published in the German publication "Bunte," in which they discussed their romantic movement. This was absolutely one of the most intriguing stories to come out in 2019. There were photographs taken of Heche and Thomas walking hand in hand while they were at the after-party for the Tribeca Film Festival. PEOPLE's TV was informed by a source close to the situation that it was very exciting news. All in the name of love, they attended a plethora of other high-profile events in the community. They both collaborated on the HBO sequel "Hung," in which Thomas played the role of Ray Drecker, an impoverished single father who resorts to prostitution in order to provide for his child. The film was directed by David Fincher. Despite the fact that they had shared a scene in Hung, it would be quite some time before they established a more meaningful connection with one another. Their efforts were fruitless because one of the most essential components that they required in order to be successful was missing from the equation.

- **Lindsey Adams Buckingham**

Lindsey Buckingham of Fleetwood Mac, who was a singer at the time, is often cited as having been the subject of one of her initial relationships that the media investigated. Just one year passed between the two of them before they broke up. Lindsey Adams Buckingham is an American musician, singer, songwriter, and producer. He is best known for his time spent as lead guitarist and as one of the vocalists for the band Fleetwood Mac between the years 1975 and 1987, as well as between 1997 and 2018. Buckingham was born on October 3, 1949. Buckingham has released three solo albums in addition to the six solo albums and three live albums he has released during his time with Fleetwood Mac. He was inducted into the Rock and Roll Hall of Fame in

1998 as part of Fleetwood Mac, which earned him the honor. Buckingham was given the position of 100 on the list of "The 100 Greatest Guitarists of All Time" that was published in Rolling Stone Magazine in 2011. Fingerpicking is a style of guitar playing that Buckingham is famous for. Buckingham received the majority of his early exposure through the band Fleetwood Mac, which dates back to the late 1960s and was initially a British blues outfit fronted by Peter Green. Buckingham joined Fleetwood Mac in 1973. After Green left the band, they went through some rough times because they lacked a consistent frontman for many of those years. In 1974, Buckingham was extended an invitation to become a member of the band because they had previously worked together in the recording studio. Additionally, the band lacked a guitarist and a male lead vocalist at the time. Buckingham made the inclusion of Stevie Nicks in the band an essential condition for the band's formation. Nicks is both Buckingham's romantic and musical partner. Buckingham and Nicks became Fleetwood Mac's public faces during the band's most commercially successful period, which was highlighted by the release of the multi-platinum album Rumors, which has sold more than 40 million copies around the world. Buckingham left the band in 1987 to concentrate on his solo career despite the fact that the band had achieved a great deal of commercial success but was plagued by almost constant internal creative and personal conflict. Buckingham performed some vocals on one track of their 1995 album Time, and he rejoined the band full-time in 1997 for the live tour and album The Dance. Some rapprochement between the former band members was initiated by a one-time reunion that took place in 1993 at the inauguration ball for President Bill Clinton. Buckingham was dismissed from his position with Fleetwood Mac without warning on April 9, 2018, and was succeeded by Mike Campbell and Neil Finn. In 2019, Buckingham had surgery to open his chest and repair his heart. Lindsey claimed that the song Down on Rodeo, which he wrote in 2006, was about his relationship with Anne Heche.

CAR CRASH AND HEALTH UPDATE

The news of Anne Heche's accident broke on Friday, and the Internet immediately went into a frenzy as a result. People are searching the internet for information regarding Anne Heche's health and her recent car accident. On August 5, 2022, Anne Heche was involved in multiple car accidents in the Mar Vista neighborhood of Los Angeles, which is located in California. The first accident occurred when her car collided with a garage that was attached to an apartment around the corner. During the second one, she was involved in a collision with a house. which led to a serious fire breaking out, which came dangerously close to taking her life. Heche was in immediate need of rescue, so personnel from the fire department and the ambulance service rushed to the location. She was transported from the scene of the accident directly to the hospital, where she arrived there in a critical condition. On the seventh, her friend, Heather Duffy Boylston provided the Associated Press with an update on her condition, stating that she was in a stable condition and making progress, despite suffering from serious burn injuries. The law enforcement agencies told the Los Angeles Times that Anne was under the influence of alcohol at the time of the car accident, and that she was also being careless. According to Brian Humphrey, one of the firefighters, the structural damage caused by Anne's crash into the house was extensive. And in order to put an end to the blaze and save Anne, it required approximately 59 firefighters and 1 hour and 5 minutes of their time. When the car crashed into the house, fortunately, the homeowner was not present, and as a result, did not sustain any injuries. After the accident, the most recent information regarding Anne's health indicates that she is currently in a coma and has not regained consciousness. During these difficult times for the actress, her family requests everyone's prayers and asks for everyone's assistance. James, Anne's ex-boyfriend, has expressed his hope that she will recover quickly and has told the Daily Mail that Anne is a resilient woman who will prevail despite the challenges she is facing.

ANNE HECHE

PART FOUR
MORE OF ANNE

LEGAL BATTLES

Competing lawsuits had been brought up in relation to the children's sunscreen manufacturer Tickle Time. La Bella Donna mineral makeup was first found by Heche and her business partner, James Tupper, a number of years ago. It was a foundation, a concealer, and sun protection all rolled into one, as stated on the website of the cosmetics company. Heche and Tupper were so pleased with the results of the sunblock that they decided to approach the inventors of LBD, Kathleen Tracy and Nicole Tracy-Arranaga, with the idea of developing a children's sunblock based on LBD's mineral formula. In March of 2012, they established Tickle Time, with Heche, Tupper, Tracy, and Tracy-Arranaga holding equal ownership of the company. Tickle Time's management and day-to-day operations were handled by Tracy and Tracy-Arranaga, despite the fact that Heche and Tupper had no prior expertise in the business world and had pledged to be entirely responsible for the company's marketing and publicity. The "quick friendship," however, was not destined to survive. On Tuesday, Tracy and Tracy-Arranage filed a lawsuit against Heche, Tupper, and Tickle Time, alleging that the defendants made an erroneous decision to attempt to take control of Tickle Time. On the same day, Heche and Tupper filed a countersuit against the co-founders of La Bella Donna. Heche and Tupper asserted that the Tracys had violated their contractual and fiduciary duties by engaging in self-dealing and purposefully undermining the company in order to pave the way for the introduction of their own competing product. They also included La Bella Donna as a defendant in their complaint.

In a response to her startling claims that he lost $450,000 of their money through shady deals, Heche's ex-husband, James Tupper, was quoted in court filings as accusing her of perhaps engaging in "extensive drug usage." Radar was able to secure these documents. Heche accused Tupper of attempting to sell their expensive home in Los Angeles behind her back in a covert transaction. After getting divorced, the exes at first came to an unusual agreement whereby they would each take turns living in the house during the weeks that they had custody of Atlas. This unusual arrangement was initially accepted by both parties. On the other hand, Heche asserted that the actor from Big Little Lies had broken their pledge by altering the security code and the keys. She stated that he had the intention of putting the house up for sale as well as showing it to several inspectors. Heche hurried to the courthouse in November 2019 to request an urgent judgement from the judge so that she and their kid would not be kept out of the home in the future. Tupper refuted her charges in a letter to the court that was made public and said he hadn't altered the code in decades, according to the reports.

CHARITY WORKS

On November 18th, Mr. Warburton Media hosted the 2020 annual "Kiss The Stars" event, which benefited Rhonda's Kiss Cancer Nonprofit, an organization founded by Kyle Stefanski that assists cancer patients in need with non-medical expenses. The event was also hosted by actress Anne Heche and presented by breast cancer patient reconstructive surgery specialist, Dr. Michael Newman. The breathtaking and energizing evening was hosted at the Olivetta Rooftop of the La Peer Hotel in West Hollywood. It took place beneath a sky filled with stars. Rhonda's Kiss is an organization that caters to the non-medical requirements of patients. They do this by providing grants to hospitals that are partners in the organization in order to develop patient assistance funds that are targeted exclusively toward cancer patients who are in need. The patient assistance funds, which are managed on an individual basis by each hospital, are intended to assist patients in covering the costs of rent and utilities, wigs, oncology massage, parking or other transportation costs, and any other unforeseen costs associated with providing a holistic level of care to patients.

LAST NOTE

The actress's family members, including her parents and siblings, have not always held the same perspectives on life as she does. It is said that her parents were partially responsible for the childhood trauma she experienced. Despite this, the actress persevered through the difficulties of her traumatic beginnings in order to carve out a successful career for herself. The Heche household harbored a number of secrets, some of which Anne Heche eventually revealed in her adult life. Despite the fact that Anne's pain could have only been alleviated by learning the truth, these secrets may have been buried with her. Since Anne is presently unresponsive in the hospital, all we can do is send our best wishes for a speedy recovery and keep our fingers crossed that she will soon be back on her feet.